Non Fiction
Spirit, Mind, Body
Religion, Education
WORDS (10220)

How to become A "REMNANT"

Avoid Eternal Hell

For Christians, Protestants, Atheist

By

Gloria Cannady

CONTACT: (WOPW) World Outreach Prayer Warriors
1700 NORTHSIDE DRIVE A7 #5962
ATLANTA, GA 30318
.w.o.prayerwarriors@gmail.com
https://w.o.prayerwarriors.com

HOW TO BECOME A
REMNANT
AVOID ETERNAL HELL
For Christians, Protestants
and Atheists

FIRST EDITION
GLORIA CANNADY
COPYRIGHT © 2023, 2024,

PUBLISHED BY: GLORIA CANNADY WITH
WORLD OUTREACH PRAYER WARRIORS

THANK YOU

I am very thankful to be a believer in Christ our Lord of Abraham, Issac, Jacob, and Moses. Because of the Seal of the Holy Spirit upon my tabernacle of life, I was given this testimony which is written about in this book, because of a prayer I cried to the Lord to show me my *Spiritual Heritage.* After studying my biological family heritage for 30 plus years, the next most important knowledge for me to learn was the answer to this question. The Lord's answer initially came when I was led by a prophetic word from the Lord through Prophetess Selena Byrd. I was challenged one Sunday morning to dive into the revelations that today are of monumental spiritual understanding for me and my family. This book is the answer to my divine receipt, which I share in hopes that the lives of others would be transformed in this divinely appointed time, at this age of humanity just as mine has been. The Lord sent two other friends in ministry to me at that time and I want to make note of my thanks to Patrick and Katherine Gray for introducing me to the topic of Shemitah. As well as their unwavering support of the World Outreach Prayer Warriors. I also want to thank others who were co-workers in the early days of the ministry Roslyn Booker notably, today known as (WOPW) World Outreach Prayer Warriors. I want to thank my Parents, Grandparents and ancestors of many generations for accepting the Lord and leading me to a life of salvation. I am a Remnant by choice, I confirm my choice to sell out my life to the rule of Christ.

> NOW is TIME for all believers of all the ages of humankind!

TABLE OF CONTENTS

Introduction

Many of us who have been introduced to the kingdom of the Lord through the spiritual blessings of our ancestors' obedience, came to know the Lord and believers in Christ early in life.

In my desire to have greater understanding of the bible principles and precepts, I spent many years of my life with some serious questions about the gaps of my spiritual heritage as I continued to grow in knowledge and understanding of the Lord's inspired Word. I became more confused because this country in which I was born said it was a nation set up upon the principle "In God We Trust." However, the actions it displays have never lined up with that principle. I finally did the smart thing and took the question directly to the Lord in prayer.

I have come a long way over several years in receipt of my answer. Traveling a path that has been paved with many struggles and changes which have transformed my lifestyle and my daily living, caused me to become more dependent upon the Lord rather than man.

All who will follow The Lord's commands are intended to be beneficiaries of blessings appointed for "humankind," but those blessings have conditions.

Conditions of the Blessings:

In the Book of Deuteronomy chapters 28-30 the word shows us some conditions involved in walking in and receiving The Lord's blessings which are as follows:

- Diligently listen to the voice of Our Savior.
- Use utmost endeavors to acquaint ourselves with the will of Our Savior the Lord. Observe and do all his commandments, memorial Holy Days, and feast celebrations. Walk in his ways, keep them forever.
- Do not wander either right or left, no superstition, profaning, do not go after other gods.
- Shore up your spiritual walk, practice both the form and the power, in the family and the nation, then The Lord will not fail to bless you.

By sharing the hidden revelations of the truth of the "Hebrew" genealogy, questions and confusion of members of the spiritual body of our Savior give better understanding to the scriptures. We must prepare to become the "Bride of Yashaya (hebrew) meaning our Savior," as the Lord has planned, predestined and prophesied since "In the beginning." To do this we must begin and end with the entire Word of The Lord as it is written, not as it has been given by religious sects (organizations) who want to deny the judgements it announces against all followers of evil. What Are Spiritual Blessings.

Spiritual blessings are the manifestations of supernatural occurrences, not to be mistaken as only material wealth. This is, in fact, the full awareness of the

Lord moving through your faith.

An example is the ability to dream about future events and see them happen in reality; or lay hands on the sick and they recover; or not have money for bills and money becomes available. None of these are blessings provided without spiritual intervention upon any source in the natural world.

Do not get spiritual blessings twisted with what man says it is. It is an eternal substance being revealed to the Lord's people before the natural manifestation. When we pray the Lord hears, instructs his angels appointed to each believer to act in the heavenly realm manifesting in the natural. We are promised an abundance of all good things, so we might have the wherewithal to honor our Savior and serve him cheerfully.

Plus, our Savior and Lord can command success and satisfaction overall we put our hands to do, because of our declarations in prayers, meaning accomplishment and satisfaction over our endeavors. We must never be idle, even when we are rich, we must find something worthwhile to set our hands to do, because our Savior, our Lord blesses the hands of the diligent. (Prov. 10:4) We also have a promise of honor among our neighbors if we live righteously.

The Lord our Savior will set us on high, above all nations by his covenant which we represent to the world by our properly gained outward prosperity. There is a two part promise of wealth (Thy shall lend to many nations) and power (Thy Lord shall make thee head). We shall be victorious, all who come against us shall certainly fall.

More of Spiritual Blessings;

If we seek first the Kingdom of The Lord "the spiritual" righteousness thereof, all other things shall be added unto us and the Grace of The Lord will establish us as a holy people. (Matt. 6:33).

Those who are "sincere" in holiness, our Savior promises to prove. When The Lord proves us in holiness, he thereby establishes a people to himself, for as long as we keep close to Our Savior, He will never forsake us. The Book of Proverbs sets up our reputation. "All the people of the earth shall see and know that thou art "called" by the name of Our Savior, "Yashyah"(hebrew) and that "thou are a most excellent and glorious people, under the particular care and countenance of our great Lord "I AM THAT I AM" (Ahyah Asher Ahyah)." They shall be made to know that a people called by the name "Yashyah" are without a doubt the happiest people under the sun, even during this end time when our enemies themselves are being judged over the righteous for an appointed time until and to the end of the age of humanity.

The favorites of Heaven are truly great and first or last, it will be made to appear that thou art so, if not in this world, yet at that day when those who confess our Savior now shall be confessed by him before men and angels, as those whom he delights to honor.

Now What are the Curses and Consequences?

Consequences of the curse include extreme vexation, utter ruin and eventual destruction. You can read these in detail in Leviticus 26, as well as in Deuteronomy 28:15-44.

The "curse," on the other hand, is the "dark" side

of the Cloud for those who are "disobedient". I will summarize, rather than delineate all the suffering and darkness of this very real, spiritual outcome. Those who consider choosing this destiny would be wise to read the scriptures to get clarity on their fate before making such a final rash decision. The Lord does not seek occasion against thee, nor is he apt to quarrel with thee. These curses come from one's own poor choices.

If we refuse to hear the voice of the Savior as if it were not worth heeding, and/or if we disobey or refuse to observe His written or oral commandments, we are rebelling against him.

When we reject the Savior because of the wickedness of our doings, slighting and forsaking Him, all the curses written in the Word shall come and overtake us, no matter how hard we attempt to escape them. This is as much of a promise as the blessings are and cannot be taken lightly.

The prophecies of David and the Revelation of John are not to be excluded when studying blessings and curses. If we want to live the fullness of the life the Lord has promised all humanity, and want the Remnant blessing, we must make the choice to be obedient to all of The Lord's Word, including giving honor to His celebrations.

GLOSSARY OF TERMS

Abraham: Biblical patriarch; founder of Hebrew nation; "Father of many" (Hebrew).

Adar: (February/March) Hebrew month of the Hebrew year.

Believer: (aka. Body of Our Savior; Society of Believers): All those who believe in Christ.

Yashayah: the Son of The Lord (I Am That I Am).

Apocrypha - ancient bible books written between 200B.C. and 400 A.D.

Day of Atonement: Command of repentance.

Declare: To proclaim, to remember, to activate.

Essenes: believers who refused to be associated with the Sadducees and Pharisees. Went to live alone. Said to be the disciples of our Savior.

Feast of Trumpets: (Shofar) Celebration which remembers the foretelling of the judgment by Christ upon the devil and wicked upon his return.

Feast of Tabernacle (Sukkot): Fall Feast of Booths to remember the tents The Lord provided for a dwelling after Egypt Exodus; symbol of life for eight days, marking the end of the agricultural harvest

Gentile: A person who is not a Hebrew or Israelite.

Ham: Noah's third son

Hebrew Bible (Scroll);: original, first version of the *Torah*(O/T Bible) written.

Hebrew Calendar: Calendar days based upon *Lunar*(evening) to lunar. *Hebrew*: Descendants of Jacob, grandson of Abraham; set up the kingdoms of Israel and Judah.

Japheth: Noah's second son

Holy Spirit: Female of   the Godhead (mother). 1Jn 5:7

Israel land mass: The Lord Preserves; (Hebrew); land promised to the father of many nations. Later taken at war to form a J/Hewish state created by the United Nations in May, 1948 religious "sect".

Jew/Hew: Hasidism, sometimes Hasidic Judaismh, Ashkenazi pronunciation "piety" is a religious sect. Those in rebellion to Mosaic laws. Also known as a revival movement in contemporary Western Ukraine during the 18th Century and spread rapidly through Eastern Europe.

Jubilee: Emancipation and restoration provided by Hebrew law as a celebration of 25 or 50 years.

Lunar: Moon to moon, the sun setting, and the first moon seen represents a new day.

Matzo: Unleavened bread.

Mow ed: A divine, appointed *time.*

Nisan: 1-2 month of the Hebrew year (April).

Noah: a Patriarch; son of Lamech *Passover* (Pesach): Eight day Festival in the Spring (April) representing the emancipation of believers from slavery/bondage in Egypt.

Pharisees: Uncertain Hebrews. ('sect," "heiress," "religious party," "community," "denomination." Separated themselves from the Levitical priesthood, who interpreted the law

differently; from the
common people of the
land.

Portals: windows for travel
by Angels between Heaven
and Earth;

according to Sun cycles in
creating months on 30 day
cycles, and each According
to a 364 day cycle year;
Spring, Summer, Fall and
Winter.
Publican: One who farmed
taxes to be levied from a town
or district. Mostly Hewish of
Esau's descendants
Shavuot:
Weeks
(Hebrew).
Shem: Noah's
first son.
Shemitah (Schimta):
Release (Hebrew);
Biblical sabbatical
every seventh year.
Sivan: (June) 6th month of the
Hebrew year.

Tishri: (September) 7th

(uncertain)
Remnant: Those of
Jacob's 12 Sons
tribes and Gentile
converts will return
to the Lord. Malachi
3:16-18; Rom. 9:27
Sabbath (Shabbat): A Holy
day of religious observation.

month of the Hebrew
year.
Trumpet ("Yovel"):
Rams horn.
Yashyah: (Hebrew)
My Savior.
Ahayah Ashar
Ahayah : Name in
Hebrew for the Lord,
I Am That I Am.

A REMNANT (Isa.10: 20, 21)

IS PROPHESIED TO BE THE NUMBER!

YOU HOPE TO JOIN THE HEAVENLY?

How?

STEP ONE - *Learn Your Prophetic Spiritual Heritage*

STEP TWO - *Learn Prophetic Holy Times and Seasons*

STEP THREE - *Learn Prophetic Holy Traditions and Celebrations*

STEP FOUR - *Awaken from the Valley of Dry Bones and Live A Renewed Life*

STEP FIVE - *Confess, Repent and Get Baptized*

Chapter 1

ORIGINS OF THE "HEBREW" &

"ISRAELITE TRIBES"

The Big story of the Bible is that according to II Tim 3:16 All Scripture is sacred - It is the guidance for all creation which the Lord named Humanity and provided instructions in the form of commandments, statutes and ordinances to guide his creation. The moral standards by which future promises would be delivered to "Hebrews and Israelite Tribes" and later Gentile convert origins are outlined here so let's begin...

Genealogy From Shem to Abraham:

- Gen 11:26-32 Shem at age 100 fathered Arpachshad and lived 500 years Arpachshad at age 35 fathered Shelah and lived 403 years.
- Shelah at 30 fathered Eber and lived 403 years. Eber at 34 fathered Peleg and lived 430 years. Peleg at 30 fathered Reu and lived 200 years. Reu at age 30 fathered Serug and lived 207 years.
- Serug at age 30 fathered Nahor and lived 200 years.
- Nahor at age 29 fathered Terah and lived 119 years.
- Terah at age 70 fathered Abram and lived 205 years.

Why have the words "Hebrew" "Israelite" been reduced and Christian, Protestant and Atheist been supplanted by those who have the truth but chose to hide the original hebrew scriptures until now.

This story begins with..

Abram an Hebrew Israelite, whose name means "Father of Many," a Biblical Patriarch married to Sarai and our link to our spiritual heritage as the Hebrew Israelite nation.

Abram, the Son of Terah, the brother of Nahor and Haran. He lived in Chaldea, which in Hebrew was "Kasdim," or the Southern portion of Babylonia on the right bank of River Euphrates, the area now called "Mugheir/Mugaypr"(Arab) (Gen. 11:27).

Euphrates is first mentioned in Gen. 2:14 as one of the rivers of Paradise. It is next mentioned in connection with the covenant which The Lord entered into with Abraham (Gen. 15:18), when The Lord promised Abraham's descendants the land from the river of Egypt to the river Euphrates (Deut. 11:24; Josh. 1:4). This covenant promise was fulfilled in the extended conquests of David (2 Sam. 8:2-14; 1 Chr. 18:3; 1 Kings 4:24). It was then the boundary of the kingdom to the north-east.

From Jacob (Gen. 32:28) existed the Northern Kingdom of Hebrew Israelites which included 10 of the 12 tribes, one of which was the tribe of Ephraim, whose capital city was Samaria. Over 2700 years ago, the Assyrians exiled the ten tribes of the Kingdom of Hebrew and Israelite Tribes. "In the ninth year of Hoshea, the king of Assyria captured Samaria and he carried them away to Assyria and placed them in Halah, and on the Habor, the river of Gozan, and in the cities of Medes."

Hidden Hebrews and Israelite Tribes History that is now being released to allow truth to favor the Lord's people....In the years 722-721 BC, the ten tribes who comprised the Northern Kingdom of Ancient Eden, also known as N.E. Eden was divided into the Nile Delta (Lower Egypt=Capital, Samaria) (Upper Egypt=from Cairo to Sudan)

and the ten tribes of Hebrew Israelites supposedly have never been seen since and successful attempts have been made to hide them from existence known today as modern Syria and Iraq.

It is interesting to note that in modern day N.E. Africa later called the Middle East a great many of middle east religious sects are careful to celebrate the Shabbat as A Day of Rest.

The Lord has released his revelation concerning the lost tribes. The importance of those of us who are believers being obedient to this shift is that it represents correction the Lord desires of us.

More on this later. The first version of the Words given by the Lord were written in Hebrew on scrolls for the first generation societies. These truths were later transcribed by the Greek and called Septuagint.

Gen. 12:1-3; 14:13 the Hebrew Israelite nations are based upon Abram from Ur Chaldeans.

He was considered an Immigrant Pilgrim.

Gen. 3:15 Why Abram, because he was meek and willing to follow the Lord. (Gen 10:5) His ancestral family was from Shem who was one of the sons of Noah.

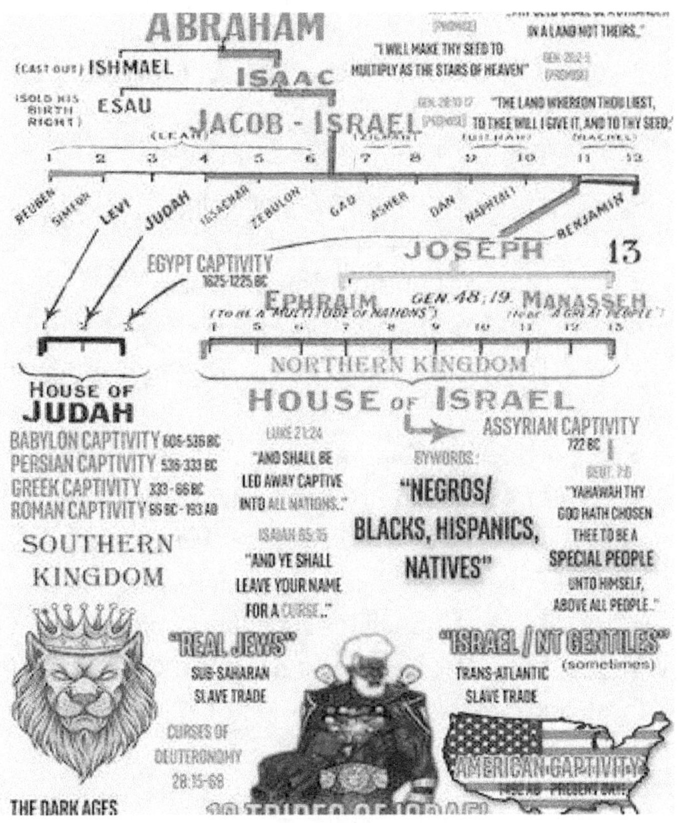

Illustration I

The Hebrew and Israelite Tribes traditions in I Kings 3:16-28 guides readers through the Kingship and Covenant periods of life.

Fact: REVELATION Twelve Tribes of Jacob/Israel not lost from Biblical Text The Remnant

Twelve Tribes of Jacob/Israel descendants today are as follows:

- Tribe of Judah - Hebrew of USA
- Tribe of Benjamin -Jamaicans
- Tribe of Levi - Hatians
- Tribe of Ephirim - Puerto Ricans
- Tribe of Manasseh - Cubans
- Tribe of Simeon -Hebrew/Brown Dominican Rep.
- Tribe of Zebulon - Mayans Panama Canal
- Tribe of Gad - Native Indians Americas
- Tribe of Asher - Brazilians/Venezuelans
- Tribe of Issachar - Mexican Brown
- Tribe of Napthali - Hawiian/Samoan
- Tribe of Dan- said to be part of Gad and Napthali located in Iran/Iraq territory

It is prophesied that the Lord had not forgotten his covenant with Abraham's descendants which he promised would be permanent, because of their sins and rebelliousness. Hosea 1:1-9.

The Bible declares in Hosea 1:10 that the descendants of the ten tribes of Israel would not die out nor be lost but would grow in population to the point they could scarcely be numbered. Gen 21:12 Hosea 1:11 prophesied a Divine Blessing would be upon the TEN TRIBES OF Jacob (ISRAEL) exiled to the Eastern Mediterranean Phoenician empire not a lost people.

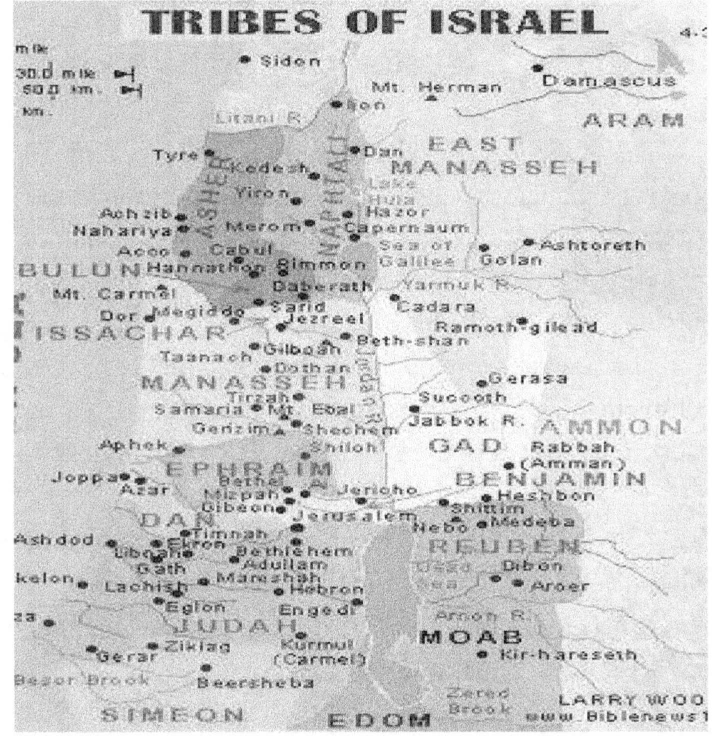

Illustration II

The ten tribes of Jacob were led by Ephriam and Manasseh according to Gen. 48:8-22. Judah remained in the land.
HIDDEN Authored books also provide favor upon the Hebrew Israelite descendants..

The Hidden Books of the Bible that were inspired by and written for the Hebrews and Israelite Tribes nations originally, to complete the story of their Spiritual Pilgrimage from the heavenly paradise would lead them to a new Jerusalem Paradise as Remnants Heb. 11:13-17.

The biblical apocrypha denotes the collection of apocryphal ancient books which were written sometime between 200 BC and 400 AD. Some Christian Churches include some or all of the same texts within the body of their version of the Old Testament.

The Books belonged to the Hebrew Israelite nations to complete the story of their Spiritual Pilgrimage from and back to the heavenly paradise Heb. 11:13-17. Remnants

I & II ESDRAS – Is a Greco-Latin

TOBIT – Comes from the Hebrew word *TOVIYAH* meaning "GOD IS GOOD" a popular hebrew male given name.

JUDITH (Extension of *ESTHER*) - A version in summary of *ESTHER* same scenarios.

WISDOM OF SOLOMON – Son of David wrote Proverbs and Eccles..

BARUCH - A Hebrew of the Tribe of Judah, a writer for Jeremiah's letters.

I & II MACCABEES - A Hebrew word for "Hammer" was the priestly family variation of the name of the Hebrew Ezra a scribe of Mattathias a Hebrew and son of John, who was the son of Simeon.

Mattathias had five sons: John, Simon, Judas, Eleazar and Jonathan who led the rebellion against those who caused destruction of the temple of Jerusalem with Hellenism being practiced against the commands, statutes and ordinances of the Lord in the state of Judah which was committed to obedience in following the Lord's ways.

These books are important to understand the war between good Angels and evil fallen Angels, still happening in both the physical earthly satanic ruling empires against the descendant tribes of the Lord. The prophecy of the return of our Savior who will destroy the wicked and grant the eternal promise to the Remnant for inheritance of the earthly peace and eternal dwelling. Today we should be living the word found in Col. 3:10 "Put on the new man which is renewed in knowledge that the Kingdom would properly be represented in the earth."

KNOW YOUR SPIRITUAL ANCESTRY

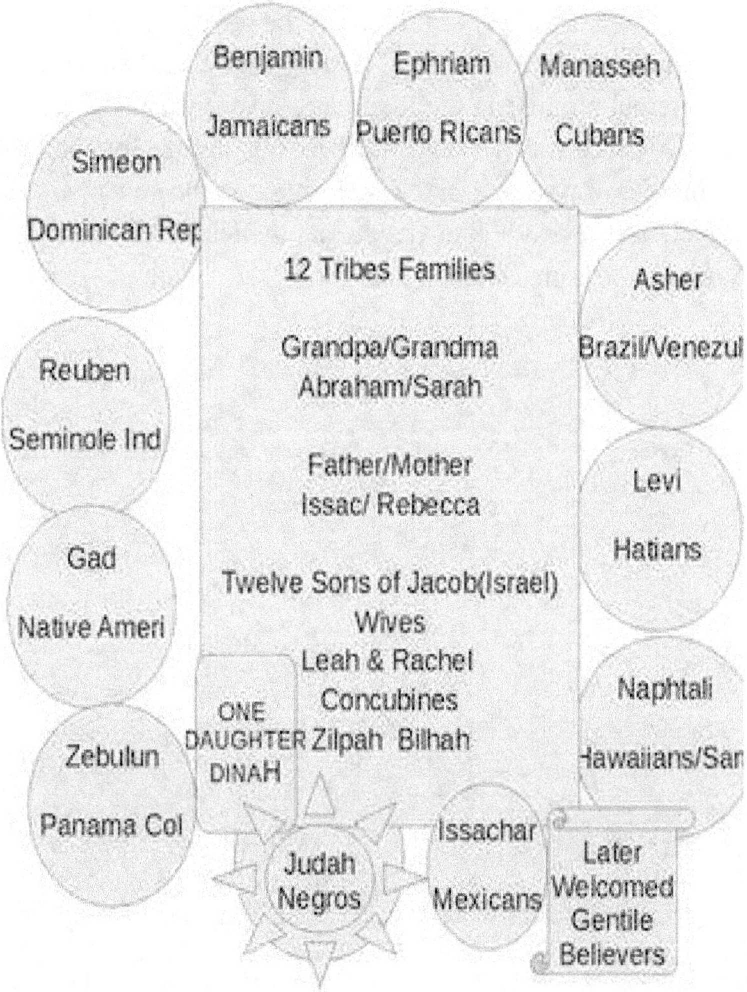

Illustration III

Chapter 2

HEAVENS TIMES, DAYS, MONTHS & YEARS

Let's begin with The Book of Enoch

Those known as Essenes wrote this book and preserved the Dead Sea Scrolls of original Hebrew Mosaic instructions. These were Hebrews and Israelite Tribes from the Levitical Priesthood who retreated to the Qumran Caves when Jerusalem was being destroyed and disobedience was ruling.

This was a place used to keep worn-out sacred writings. The Book of Enoch is confirmed by the Holy Bible in the book of Hebrews 11:5 "Enoch was translated so he would not see death. Enoch was Noah's grandfather, so these prophecies were given before the flood by the Lord. Also, Jude 1:14, you find Disciples quoting Enoch, the Wandering Stars, the Fallen Angels said to have come down on Mt. Hermon "Osirus". So it is clear why the devil worshiping religious sects/ groups would prefer these books of truth never be revealed.

The Lord has given details in Genesis 1:14; (1)for signs

for Sabbaths, Holy Days, and Jubilees. Jubilees which represent a year, also called "weeks" equal to a "year." A year multiplied by 7 equals a Jubilee totalling 49 years. This is to be celebrated the following year at the 50th year for the Lord's "Jubilee Year";

(2) Signs so his people would know how to follow his seasons, years, and days throughout all generations of believers in the earth. Sabbaths will be discussed again later. According to the book of Numbers 23:9 The Lord did not want his people to take deceptive Gentile methods and associate them with True Holiness.

Next, heavenly defined hours in each day outlined:

According to the Words of Genesis 1:5; - each day begins at "Lunar(evening)" and was created using the formula that 80 parts(minutes) =per one hour cycle. According to the hour cycles of the Sun in and out of the heavens "portals".

Finally, the Winter days of Sun and Moons leading to the New Year are equal parts to the Sun and Moon at the end of each year, this would zero out at a new year beginning.

The Lord has given instructions to keep confusion from interfering with the establishing of the days so that there would be clarity about when the memorials, feast days, jubilees and preservation of his laws, statutes and commands could continue to be performed according to his calendar. ENOCH 72:1 The angel Uriel in accordance with instructions from the Lord was commanded to teach all to follow Holy days throughout eternity. Psalms 24:1 "The earth is the Lord's and the fullness therein..."

v.3 who shall ascend (go out) ... hill; who shall stand in his Holy place, v.7 Angelic Leaders over the gates..., v. 8-10 The Lord has Hebrews and Israelite Tribes nations leaders over .... Psalm 24:3 Only Jacob's sons have this opportunity to travel through the portal Psalms 48:1-2 in Mt. Hermon today Mt Zion, Syria.

Why Is the Sabbath an important command?

According to Gen 1:14 the Sabbath is a sign from the Lord to his people to remain obedient to honoring this Holy day as the "Day of Rest". Hebrew days are evening to evening aka lunar to lunar.

Hebrew Weekly Days to Sabbath

Secular Weekday Name	Hebrew Name	Hebrew Order day begins eve to eve
Sunday	First day	First day
Monday	Second day	Second day
Tuesday	Third day	Third day
Wednesday	Fourth day	Fourth day
Thursday	Fifth day	Fifth day
Friday	Fifth/Sixth day/eve	Fifth/Sixth day/eve
Saturday	Sabbath	Day of Rest

The Lord's calendar as was shown to Enoch:

Let's begin with the Sun's purpose and movement defined according to the Heavenly Realm, which consist of "12 portals". The moon's purpose and movement according to 30 days per month and three months from season to season.

Illustration V

Portals created for Sun and Moon cycles

Portals are designed as windows for the travel by angels between heaven and earth according to Sun cycles. Months are designed in 30 day cycles which results in a 364 day annual cycles.
The cycles are the result of the four seasons of Spring, Summer, Fall and Winter. According to the words given to Enoch by the Lord himself.

Chapter 3

WHAT IS SHEMITAH?

THE NUMBER SEVEN COVENANT

SOUNDING THE TRUMPET - TRADITION OF THE HEBREW?

"Shemitah" is a Hebrew word which means "release," a "Mow-ed," which is hebrew for a "divinely appointed time" set by The Lord. The Shemitah principle of seven Year Sabbaticals was established to bring order to the wealth building of land and agriculture development which have always been commodities of vital importance to the rulership of empires since the beginning of humanity.

Also, this principle is a key measure of the moral and spiritual obedience necessary for peaceful co-existence upon the earth. "The govt. will be upon ... the shoulders of our Savior." Isaiah 9:6
The English translation of Shemitah is in Leviticus 23:23-25 we find that the Lord gives detailed instruction and direction for how He wanted His people to live both before and after the Flood. This includes the Exodus (Passover) and twelve Tribes of Israel/Jacob's descendants after the Holocaust of oppression and Slavery. The patriarchs and matriarchs and all descendants of Abraham, Issac and Jacob are still dedicated to this principle. Throughout the generations oppressed Israelite believers could choose to remain in a bond status of living.

The Lord also set this time for all Israelite believers, to teach us to depend upon the Lord's provisions.

The Lord shows his power, thereby helping us to be reminded of the faith we must use in depending upon his Divine provisions.

It is also known that Shemitah marks the beginning of a prophetic series of events that would culminate in the prophecy about the "Coming of Christ" season.

Sevens Covenant Sabbatical Years

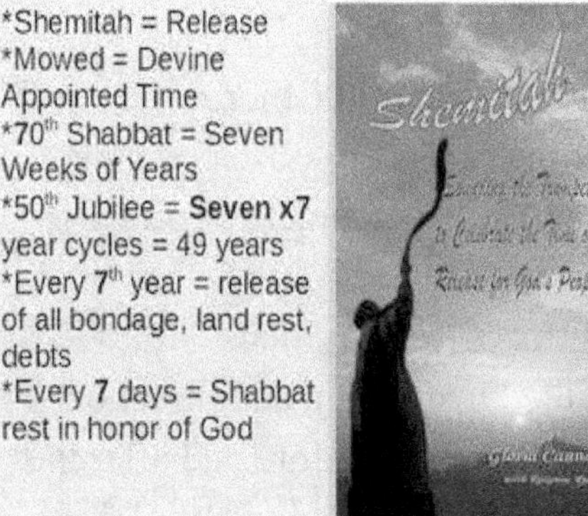

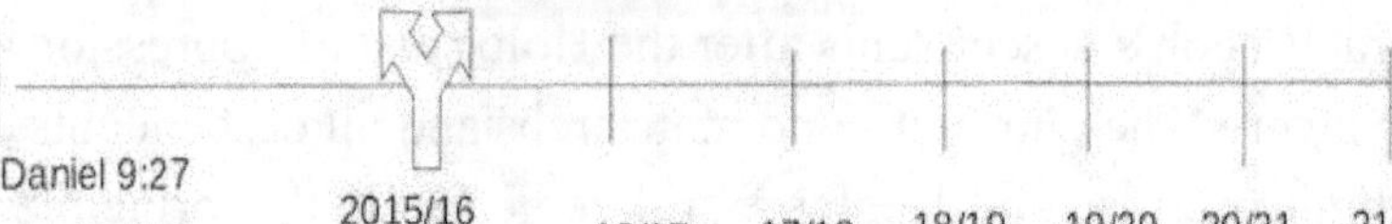

The Truth from The Book of Jubilees;

Sounding the Trumpet

The importance of this book is it supplies the history of the division of days using the number seven. It gives the laws regarding the Jubilees.
The Lord has given details in Genesis 1:14 (1) signs for Sabbaths, Holy Days, Jubilees which represent 7 years/weeks (7 year/week= 7 years) a total of 49 years is a Jubilee which signals the 50th celebration between the Lord and his people and; (2) Signs so his people would know how to follow his seasons, years, and days throughout all the years of humanity in the world.

The knowledge and understanding about Shemitah is also found in the book of Josephus Book 1, Chapter 2 v. 3- 4.

Based on the Word of the Lord, the beginning of this divine appointed time is designated as the beginning count to the years of humanity after the flood. In order to count the Jubilees, one must know how to count heaven's years thereby understanding the Shemitah Sevens Covenant.

REVELATION: The Year of our Lord (5775/76) 2015/16 is when the Lord exposed me to this revelation. This Marked the Seventieth (70th) Jubilee according to Lev. 23:23-25; Numbers 29:1-6; Exodus 23:16 and Deut. 15:1-18. Hebrew male/female all are to remember this statute. Every seven years the Sabbatical Covenant requires the Rest, Restoration and Release of all servants "Hebrews" and "Israelite Tribes" responsibilities, debts and wealth being unjustly held from those in servitude. My theory is satan's futile effort was implementing the bankruptcy laws. Rather than obedience to the Lord, to restore and return all slaves to status held before servitude.

NOTE: As it was commanded by Noah of all his sons to live a neighborly existence in the land after he divided their lots. Noah charged them to not rule over one another. I now know that this statute was broken by Nimrod and resulted in sin and judgment that would become the punishment for breaking the norm of peaceful existence within societies until the end of time of the age of humanity, Christ returns to re-establish his New Jerusalem for Remnants to dwell as it was before.

This count of sevens (days, years) gave me relevance, commitment and motivation to learn to live according to the ancient Hebrew calendar, and I now know I am reaping the blessings of obedience with new spiritual exercise in understanding, new power and fear of the Lord. I have more days of peace and less stress now. Rev. 1:4, 3:1, 4:4, 5:6 KJV As I continue in my learning there are several books that I had to get to confirm the answers to missing information in my spiritual ancestry story. These hidden books are key to clarity of some of my questions as the Lord continues to lead me to his answers to my question. Col. 3:10 "Put on the new man which is renewed in knowledge that the Kingdom would be properly represented in the earth."

Again I had to get real about understanding the wars that came about against the ruling empires which sought to kill all devout practicing "Hebrews" and "Israelite Tribes" of which I am connected by bloodline.

The devil and his followers since Essau and Jacob and before have sought to prevent anyone from living up to and according to the commands, statutes and ordinances established by the Word of Lord for all humanity.

The most important take-aways from this chapter I pray you receive are:
The Lord set this time for the Seven Year Shemitah covenant to teach us to depend upon him and his providence for his creations.

His command that all land, persons in bondage and oppressed unjustly be made whole if they chose to leave the bondage every seven years. A restart was the command so that all "Israelite Tribes" and today.

Gentile converts are given access to all of the land according to the ancient Hebrew calendar, and I now know a Remnant of all 12 Tribe Nations will inherit the earth eventually reaping the blessings of obedience with greater earthly resources and dwell in peace.

I repeat the foundation of the Lord's promises are found in Exodus 34.

"…Then Moses climbed Mount Nebo from Jericho. There the Lord showed him the whole land promised from Gilad to Dan, all of Naphtali, the territory of Ephraim and Manasseh. All the land of Judah as far as the Mediterranean Sea, the Negev and the whole region from the valley of Jericho, the city of Palms as far as Zoar. The Lord said to him, this is the land I gave to Abraham, Issac and Jacob.

The Lord's defense on our behalf is the bible as it was written about us and for us that is why the hatred by the Synagogue of Satan and his followers. This explains the unexplainable experiences that have confused me all my life. Why the saints, obedient ones suffered so in the societies ruled by the devil's followers. Ten empires prophesied to go before the return of Christ and each has oppressed and sought to kill "Hebrews and Israelite Tribes", Thank the Lord for his creation and restoration for his chosen people for his appointed time. Acts 1:7 "No man knows when our Savior will return, … return he will rule and we will dwell in peace.

Chapter 4

THE ANNUAL HIGH HOLY DAYS, MEMORIALS AND

FESTIVALS OF THE LORD

"CARGO CARRIERS"

In writing this chapter, I reflect on those Hebrew citizens the Lord created to be the "Cargo Carriers" throughout the world.
Spiritually blessed people of the Lord have suffered for the sake of the gospel.

Believers have been forced off the Land that they planted, picked and from which they harvested the crops that have built the wealth for societies of the world. This is a way to remember how much the Lord loves us, that he entrusted our ancestors' faith in that way (See Ex. 34:22; Num. 26, 28, 31; Deut. 16:9-12; Acts w:1-4)

The chart below shows the annual festivals commanded by the Lord. In biblical reckoning, days that begin in the evening (Genesis 1:5), when the sun goes down (Joshua 8:29; 2 Chronicles 18-34, Mark 1:32, and are counted "from evening to evening" (Leviticus 23:32). Thus, all The Lord's festivals begin at sunset just before the dates listed in the table on the facing page. According to the Hebrew Calendar, Springtime Begins Each New Year We cannot know when to celebrate, remember and memorialize Holy times according to the Bible without knowledge of the Hebrew calendar.

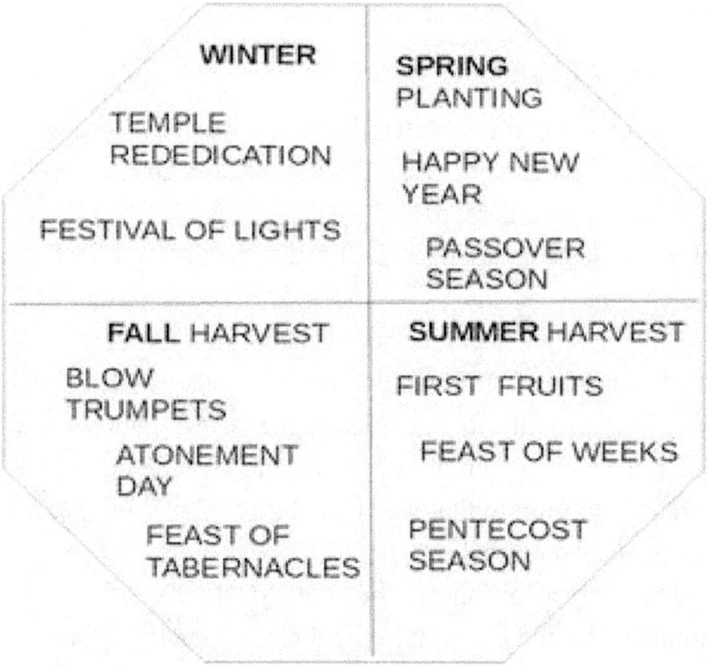

Illustration VIII

Rev. 7:1 tells of Angels on the four corners of the earth setting off the season of judgment against the haters of the Lord.

Why Is the Sabbath an important discussion?

Sabbath The First "Holy Day"

According to Gen 1:14 the Sabbath is a sign from the Lord to his people to remain obedient to honoring this Holy day as the "Day of Rest"

Secular Weekday Name	Hebrew Name	Hebrew Order day begins eve to eve
Sunday	First day	First day
Monday	Second day	Second day
Tuesday	Third day	Third day
Wednesday	Fourth day	Fourth day
Thursday	Fifth day	Fifth day
Friday	Fifth/Sixth day/eve	Fifth/Sixth day/eve
Saturday	Sabbath	Day of Rest

illustration IX

TRADITIONS OF THE FOUR SEASONS

The Lord commanded Moses and Aaron that they declare the Exodus Passover in Caanan, the land upon which The Lord established the " New Year " which was to be the believers' new year forever.

They obeyed, and Joshua continued the practice, so that we as believers and beneficiaries today may continue to live these commands as well.

According to the Hebrew calendar, the first day of the first month is identified as Adar (March) First.

This time also marks the beginning of another "Seven Year Sabbatical," another significant counting of the release of the land, as well as of those under bondage to personal debt (the Shemitah we have been referring to) command regarding the seven year rest, and restoration.

This is equivalent to a New Harvest, New Land, New Beginning, and New Groups of Believers. In James 1:18, he references "all believers" as the first- fruits of The Lord's work since the birth, death and resurrection of Our Savior that was given by the word of truth (see also Leviticus 23:15).

KNOW YOUR **BIBLICAL SEASONS** SAITH THE LORD

Illustration X

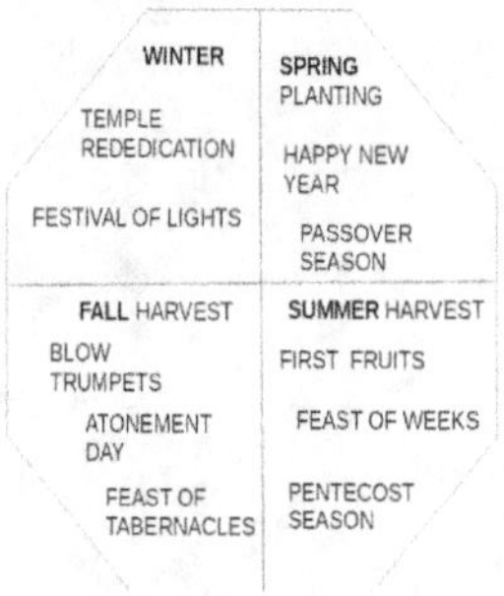

- **NEW YEAR & PASSOVER**
- **UNLEAVENED BREAD**

The Lord commanded Moses, Joshua and Aaron that a Passover Sabbath be performed. This is a yearly spiritual ceremony for the Body of Our Savior which represents his first fruits as his Body/Bride. In accordance with The Lord's Word, we must recognize and celebrate our Passover on 14 Adar/Nisan (Mar/April), the 14th day of the first month of the Hebrew calendar year, followed by a Passover Seder on the 15th. Strict rituals apply to this celebration. This ritual feast is in remembrance of the slaughter of the first-born in every Hebrew household except those in Rahab's home. by King Hored

Passover Seder

The Passover Seder, the most commonly celebrated of Hebrew rituals, is a feast that marks the beginning of the Hebrew holy day of Passover. It is conducted on the evening of the 14th/15th of Adar/Nisan throughout the world. This corresponds to March/April in the Gregorian calendar.
The Seder is a tradition performed by a community or by multiple generations of a family, involving a retelling of the story of the liberation of the Hebrew and Israelite Tribes from bondage in ancient Egypt. This story is in the Book of Exodus in the Bible.

Traditionally, families and friends gather in the evening to read the text, which contains the narrative of the Israelite exodus from Egypt, offering special blessings and special Passover songs.

Seder customs include telling the story, discussing the story, drinking four cups of wine, eating matzo, partaking of symbolic foods placed on the Passover Seder Plate, and reclining in celebration of freedom.

Feast of Unleavened Bread

The Lord also commanded that a Pilgrimage Feast be performed to begin the day after the Passover which symbolizes a remembrance of the quick movement when leaving Egypt that left no time for waiting for yeast to rise as normal in preparing bread. Also symbolized the release from the manna(food) they were required to live on while in the wilderness until the return to a rich diet in the new land of milk and honey. The "Feast of Unleavened Bread" is celebrated for seven days. This pilgrimage feast commences on the Sabbath of Adar/March after Passover and ends on the Sabbath eight days later Adar/March. See Exodus 23:14-17, Leviticus 23-25; and Deuteronomy 16:16.

Since many of our Kingdom believers do not acknowledge Biblical feasts, they remain unaware of the blessings attached to the observance of the feasts. In the case of Pesach Sheni, The Lord has allowed a second chance for His people to observe the feast celebration and receive the blessing!

Pesach Sheni – The Lord's 'Second Passover' Pesach Sheni literally means "Second Passover" and was instituted in the Law to provide an opportunity for those who were unable to participate in the Passover earlier. Some of the men approached Moses and Aaron and were concerned that they were going to be deprived of the chance to be right with The Lord.

They asked what should be done, and in response, The Lord allowed for a "second chance" for the celebration of the Passover a month later. This celebration would take place on one day instead of seven.

The celebration of a second Passover finds its roots in the teaching of the scriptures. The Lord instructed the Israelites to remember the night of Passover when the death angel passed over any Hebrew home that had been sprinkled with the lamb Savior's blood. This occurs every year of Adar/Nissan (March/April) month of the Hebrew calendar.

COME CELEBRATE OUR HOLY PASSOVER & DELIVERANCE

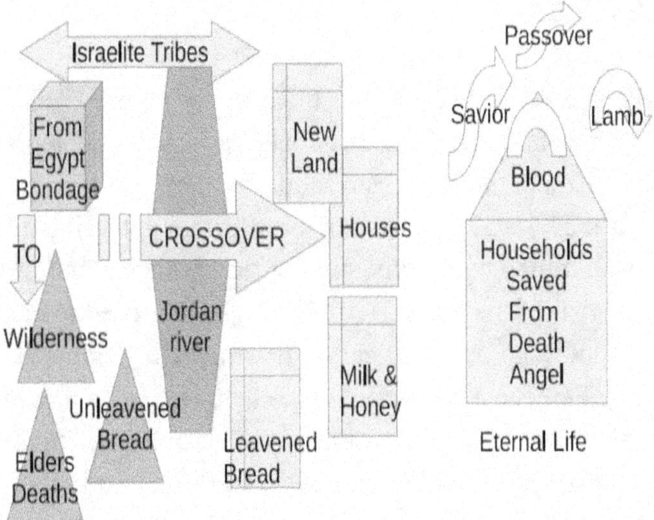

New Testament Hebrew 5-6 – Christ Ashayah our Savior
represents the sacrificed lamb which atoned for our sins as
our High Priest.
Matt.5:17-18; 26:17-18 Sabbath Shabbat is the Holy Day
Galatians 4:4-7

SUMMER CELEBRATIONS

- **PENTECOST**
- **FEAST OF WEEKS (SHAVOUT)**

PENTECOST

Pentecost, well known by many in the Body of our Savior, to mean "Fifty" in the Greek, because it is celebrated 50 days also counted as seven sabbaths after Passover. (Leviticus 23:15-22) This is the least formal gathering of all the feasts. It may have something to do with the significance of the arrival of the comforter which was promised to come what we know to be the impartation of the Holy Spirit.

The Pentecost celebration is to be treated as a day of spiritual convocation. A great holy worship, filled with praise, preaching, teaching and reading of the Lord's word. The celebration would include a feast together in remembrance of the receiving of the Holy Spirit to give heaven's guidance in the earth since Christ went back to dwell in heaven and cover our fallen state before the Lord.

The Pentecost is also a reminder of the day of the writing of the law and the fulfillment of the Holy Spirit, which descended upon Christ after he was baptized. As we have learned, the Old Testament is filled with the laws now at the Pentecost which are to become memorized in our hearts since Christ's resurrection.

CELEBRATING: WEEKS "SHAVOUT" THE FESTIVAL OF WEEKS

This celebration occurs on the sixth day of the Hebrew month of Iyyar or May. It is one of three biblical pilgrimage festivals.

Feast of Weeks is seven weeks beginning on the second day after Passover. This counting of days and weeks is understood to express anticipation and desire for the giving of the Law, because it was when Israelites were given the law and became a nation committed to serving the Lord.

The festival of weeks is celebrated with a festive meal and all night study of the reading of the book of Ruth. The eating of dairy products and decorations of greenery. The book of James 1:18, references "All believers" as the First-Fruits of Christ work and the Lord's First Fruit is of course Christ himself before and after the birth, death and resurrection of our savior as was given by the word of truth. (see also Leviticus 23:15). This celebration is in remembrance of the first harvest after the Spring agriculture planting season. The perfect will of the Lord in the First Fruit of all creation.

Illustration XIII

Illustration XIV

- **BLOWING OF TRUMPETS**
- **DAY OF ATONEMENT**
- **FEAST OF BOOTHS/DWELLINGS"SUKKOT"**

BLOWING OF TRUMPETS: LEV. 23:23-25

Now, as we move to the celebrations of the Fall season, we again refer to the Lord's commands to Moses, Joshua and Aaron in Exodus 12.

The Lord commanded that the "Seventh Year Jubilee" be celebrated in the seventh month of the Hebrew calendar which is September/Tishrei on the 10th day. This is the beginning of Fall. The Lord commanded it be marked by the Blowing of the Trumpet for the return of all possessions, compensation for new beginnings, debt relief, and returning of servants to their families.

IIIlustration XV

This bible scripture teaches in Heb. 9:2; to get our relationships and tabernacles/ body temples in order in the Fall before the coming of our Savior "Our High Priest" of good things to come. This command is a call for each of us to seek a more perfect tabernacle of our body's temple like Christ and he being sanctified, justified and not made of the building tabernacle of the early tabernacle.

The Lord spoke to Moses commanding that on the 13th day of the seventh month September "Tishri" begins at evening/lunar "Fast" which goes until the evening lunar of the next day. Remember this would remind all Israelites and now Gentile converts to seek to get all relationships in order meaning seek to reconcile all and confess and repent as necessary.

Next examine our spiritual rank according to the standard of living and growing more Christlike to the image of the Lord's creation in his son. Examine how prepared we are to face the question regarding the "Book of Life" judgment. This is time to look at our temple with regard to our eternal opportunity to achieve Remnant rank in the eternal kingdom as redeemed heirs with Christ.

THE "FEAST OF TABERNACLES(Sukkot)" Lev. 23:33-44

The Lord spoke to Moses commanding that the beginning of the month of September/Tishri on the 18th day and for eight days beginning on the first Sabbath and ending on the following Sabbath, that all Israelites are to celebrate Sukkot or Tabernacles. The Sukkot in Hebrew is a tabernacle or booth which is a walled structure covered with plant material such as overgrowth or palm leaves.

Day 1 and 8 are the first and last days to be celebrated by the reading of Psalm 45 on the Sabbath. This Psalm is a wedding poem written to a King on the day of his wedding to a foreign woman, as we remember the symbol we represent to our Savior as our bridegroom. We also take note during this celebration marking the end of the Fall harvest. The more elaborate spiritual significance of Sukkot is that of commemorating the provisions and dependence of the people of the Lord; on all life resources from the Lord.

In modern times our provisions and dwellings have simply evolved into apartments, condos, single family homes made of brick and mortar. In bible days it was tents and booths. This law has not given excuse to any Hebrews, Israelite Tribes and Gentile converts from giving remembrance to this season. This Feast culminates with the fulfillment of "Our Savior" "Yashyah" coming back to redeem the Remnant his first fruits or Bride, as prophesied in Ezekiel 6 and Revelation 7:4-12. ALL WE LIVE TO BECOME!

According to the Lord's word all of the Hebrews and Israelite Tribes, Patriarchs and Matriarchs were living for and with the expectation of the arrival of a Savior Our Savior, Yashyah. This time is set according to the Hebrew calendar in the month of September/Tishri on the first day of the seven days of celebrating the Sukkot. This is a time to remember to rejoice in our Savior, the Lord's provision for our salvation and redemption.

We rejoice today in thankfulness. According to my own experience organizing and celebrating, the Lord showed up every gathering by sending his angels and nature was giving praise along with us. The wind would show up blowing, the leaves on the trees would wrestle by showing up, the ducks would gather around us, the sun would shine upon us the homeless would come and be fed by us, always a divine engagement kick-off to begin this High Holy Festival.

Days 2-6 should be spent in prayer and thankfulness. If you can sleep in a tent, it will make the experience more fulfilling. Precious time with the Lord alone builds a new level of faith and trust and appreciation for all we need to build trust in relying upon the Lord. This is also a time to begin a regular time to gather with family to read scriptures and break bread together.

Day 7 would be a good time to host this day of festivities with food, games, entertainment and preaching/teaching.

Day 8 - The culminating celebration at the beginning or the end of the Tabernacle Feast is demonstrated in reading of Psalm 45 a wedding poem, symbolizing to be held on Sabbath.

This is a most important time of celebration and thanksgiving for believers of all the ages of humankind. Do not miss this message thereby missing your greatest blessing.
The more elaborate spiritual significance of Sukkot is that of commemorating the provisions and the will of the Lord I Am that I Am "Ahayah Ashar Ahayah".

" BOOTH (SUKKOT)"

Illustration X

WINTER CELEBRATIONS

- **FEAST OF REDEDICATION/LIGHTS**
- **FEAST OF PURIM**

Rededication/Lights Festival John 10:22; Book of Maccabees Ch:4

BACKGROUND

This celebration was implemented by and because of the Maccabees Revolt Victory Celebration according to the Prophecy of Daniel 7 the Roman Antiochus Epiphanes represents the Third Beast of the Fourth ruling empires over the Hebrew and Israelite Tribes nations. This truth is found in the Apocrypha, Book One, Maccabees. An Israelite Hebrew named Matthias who was the son of Asamoneus was a priest who lived in Modin. Matthias had five sons whose names are: Judas, Eleazar, John, Simon and Jonathan.

Also According to the Book of Josephus: The Greek Ptoleman took over Egypt during this time 215 B.C. – 164 B.C.. The ancestral lineage of Esau called Edomite nations today are of Britain, Babylon, Gentiles ancestry etc. The Greeks attempted to destroy the Hebrews and Israelite Tribes customs and demoralize their societies. European Images in Egypt and Goshen's names were changed. Antiochus then goes to take Israel and Jerusalem, warring against them until the death of Herod.

Book Three of Josephus from Vespasian's coming to subdue the Hebrews and Israelite Tribes by Nero spans (69 yrs). To the Taking of Gamala which covers one year. Book Four from the siege of Gamala.

Book Five From the coming of Titus to besiege Jerusalem, to the great extraction of which the Hebrews and Israelite Tribes were reduced spans (6 mths.).

Book Six From the great extraction to the taking of Jerusalem by Titus covers One month. Christ wanted them to understand the importance of this Celebration regarding the Temple battles of the ancestors. More importantly in my opinion Acts 47:8 confirms a new building not made by men representing the saved ones from Jacob's ancestry even today. I Corin. 3:16 which says "We are the dwelling of the Holy Spirit." (See Day of Atonement).

Those who were known as Essenes were disgusted with the (Pharisees, and Sadducees disobedience). In resistance to the disobedience and the refusal to follow the Spirit of the law they "Essenes" moved out of Jerusalem and lived a monastic life in the desert. These were well respected Hebrews of Israelite Tribes.

The other Hebrews/Hewish referred to them as "School of Prophecy exalted with excellence of the word of the Lord. Egyptians called them healers and doctors; they had property in all the big cities and in Jerusalem. It is said that the Disciples and our Savior were the people of this group. In Maccabees 1 it was the sons of Matthias: Judas, Eleazar, John, Simon and Jonathan who drove Antiochus generals out of Judea.

Cyrene over a span (3 years). Matthew 24:1

Temple Rededication/Lights/Chanukah Festival

This Feast was instituted by the sons of Matthias in memorial and remembrance of the victory the Lord gave them over the Gentiles Esau's descendants called Edomites also known as the Synagogue of Satan today. The sons restored their sacred rites. Eleazar was crushed, destroying the elephant that the generals set up to defile the Temple. Maccabees 12:, 4:36 Judas and his brothers cleansed the temple, killed the deviled ones and destroyed their altars. Maccabees 4:52

The month of December "Caslew" in Hebrew an 8-day celebration was instituted. A return to the true worship in the temple. One candle was to burn for each day to put away the reproach of the Gentile heathen nations. The miracle of the oil that was found after the temple was destroyed which lasted them for eight days and the lights were put on all the doors.

Prior history of the wars fought by Hebrews and Israelite Tribes to keep their Society Holy and Pure as the Lord commanded; are recorded in books like Apocrypha but were not included nor allowed to be distributed to Judah(Hebrews) or other Tribes like Gad or Dan Native Americans in Daughter of Babylon aka USA. Also books were hidden and replaced by the Roman Papal/Catholic and many other doctrines today. Then taken throughout the world to misguide the Lord's people.

ILLUSTRATION XVII

37

According to the prophecy of Daniel 7:5 given about the Four Beasts that were a symbol of a Bear with three ribs which represent Babylon, Egypt and Lydia being defeated by the 2nd Empire of Persian and Medes nations. Daniel was given the prophecy because he was a Chief in Persia and Babylon. Chapter 10:5-13 Mordecai remembers a dream.

This important revelation is among other important hidden books called the Apocrypha. The Book of Esther part of which is in the (KJV) King James Version bible but also continued in Apocrypha.

Esther was a Hebrew and her slave name was Hadassah. She is the daughter of Abihail uncle to Mordecai. She was a cousin of Mordecai the son of Jair, the son of Shimei, the son of Kish, a Benjamite of the Tribe of Benjamin/Jamaican islands ancestry. Mordecai raised Esther as his daughter after she was left an orphan due to the death of her parents.

The time of this period was under King Ahasuerus during the 2nd Neo Persian Empire, his wife was Queen Vashiti at the time. Chapter 7 v.9 King Ahasuerus summoned his wife Queen Vashiti several times but she refused.

V. 20 Queen Vashiti is removed from the palace because she refused to come when summoned by the King. The King then begins a search to replace her. Mordecai brings Esther to the palace as the search for a new queen begins. Chapter 2 Esther pleased the keeper of the women who were being purified for selection by King Ahasuerus.

Esther is selected and crowned as the New Queen of the Persian and Medes Empire. King Ahasuerus gave Esther the Queen's portion.

Haman was the grandson of Esau's son Chapter 3:1. Haman became the King in the first month of April/Nisan 12th year of his reign, he cast lots(Pur) from day to day and month to month with intentions to kill all the people of the Lord Hebrews and Israelite Tribes. V. 13 King Hamman sent a letter to all provinces from India to Ethiopia to bow and reference him as King.

Chapter 3:2 Mordecai refused to bow down to King Haman. King Haman gets angry with Mordecai and wants to kill him and all the Hebrew Israelites who were also Esther's kinship. Esther and Mordecai consulted and all the Hebrew Israelite communities began to fast and cry out praying for three days to the Lord on their behalf. Chapter 6 six Mordicai overheard a plot to kill King Ahasuerus and Esther told the King about the plan giving Mordecai the credit for the information.

A Banquet was held by King Haman and King Ahasuerus was in attendance. King Haman was afraid that he was going to be killed and pleaded to Queen Esther. King Ahasuerus came into the palace where King Haman was pleading and became angry about what King Haman was doing. King Ahasuerus had King Haman removed.

Chapter (7) seven King Ahasuerus was thankful about the information and offered Esther to tell him what she wanted him to do for her. v. 3 Esther asked that the letter written by King Hamman be reversed against Mordecai and her people. The 7th year in the month of Shevat

King Ahasuerus granted Mordecai the Kingship over all the provinces from India to Ethiopia. This is the reason for this celebration. Truth being revealed behind gift giving is a welcome narrative.

According to Esther 8:13 a celebration and remembrance in the 12th month (Shevat)Feb hebrew, that is February, 13th day v.15 attire of the event is blue and white with crown of gold and fine purple linen, v. 22 remember the sorrow and the joy with gifts to the poor. Chapter 9:26, two days called "Purim" a memorial to the defeat of the enemy to the Lord's chosen Israelite Tribes and Hebrews. Chapter 10:1-3 Mordecai receives the Kingship of 120 providences all who practiced truth and obedience to the Lord. Esther is granted freedom for her Israelite Hebrew brothers and sisters.

ILLUSTRATION XVIII

Gift Giving To The Poor

120 Provinces Given to Mordeci as King by King Ahasuerus

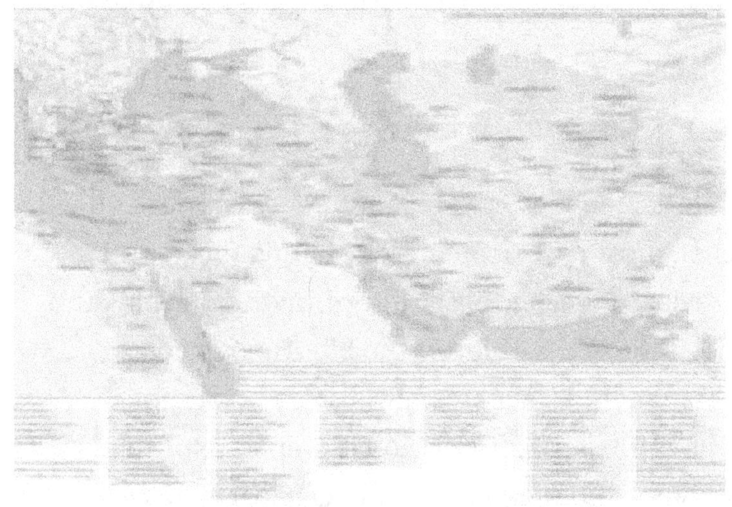

Illustration XIX

MAP OF ANCIENT ETHIOPIA TO INDIA NORTHERN KINGDOM HTTPS://MAPSONTHEWEB.ZOOM-MAPS .COM/IMAGE/170000577601

Footnote: Questions of the Feast and the Lord's commands. Bible References: I Corinthians 5:8 Let us keep the feast not with the old leaven – but with the understanding that our Savior today represents the new sacrifice. Also read Luke 1:68-73.

Note: For further information refer to www.freemaninstitute.com.

Author

Gloria Cannady is a servant, prayer warrior and teacher, most passionate about sharing the gospel of our Savior. A teacher of spiritual growth principles and enthusiastic in the study of the bible and genealogy. She has created several family history books not realizing the prophetic mission it prepared for this book. She co-founded the World Outreach Prayer Warriors in 2014.

Although she was baptized at the age of 7, when she graduated high school and became of age, like most christians in time she spent time in the dangerous playground of Satan and was drawn back to her foundation and delivered from drugs and alcohol in 1986, when she began true ministry in 1992. She has served the Lord's people under leadership and through many other local ministries.

Her roles most often included door-to-door evangelism, home-bound visitations, a choir member and family quartet participation. She helped to found and establish churches, employee self-help organizations and community non-profit organizations. She has written multiple books, computer consulting and training video production are in her skill sets. Currently she is developing content for internet platforms and podcast production. Sister Gloria holds a: Masters of Science in Education; Bachelors of Science in Business, and Associates of Applied Science in Computer Information Systems. Gloria is a divorced widow with two adult daughters and five grandchildren.

REMNANT COVENANT

I ______________________ Confess as a Convert of The Body of Christ:

Since the People of The Lord from creation to the flood, (1656 years ago according to the Hebrew text), the patriarchs who were looking for Our Savior, the new Adam. Until the end of time.

I declare that as a child of the most High King Our Savior, I will never turn from The Lord's directions and instructions because I will remember what happened to cause our Covenant leader Moses to not be able to possess the inherited promise of the land;

I declare that as a child of the most High King Our Savior, I will meditate and get understanding so the Word is ready in me at all times;

I declare that as a child of the most High King Our Savior, the sins of our third and fourth generation ancestors which held us back are now released from the curse and I will be strong and courageous.

I declare that as a child of the most High King Our
Savior, I will keep The Lord's laws, knowing that
doing so will entitle me to possess His blessings and
the desires of my heart which He has promised;
I declare that as a child of the most High King Our
Savior, I will make no exceptions when doing all that
is required, even when those laws are displeasing;
I declare that as a child of the most High King Our
Savior, I will observe the checks of conscience, hints
of providence and functions of the Holy Spirit,
appreciating the advantages these blessings bring;
I declare that as a child of the most High King Our
Savior, I will not get complacent or become idle;
I declare that as a child of the most High King Our
Savior, I will acknowledge and repent of my sins,
examining myself daily, and resolve to continually
live a renewed life;
I declare that as a child of the most High King Our
Savior, I will remember The Lord fulfilled and I can
go in to possess all that was held from us;
I declare that as a child of the most High King Our
Savior everything in my life and coming from my
mouth must line up with the word of The Lord;
I declare that as a child of the most High King Our
Savior, I will observe to do all that The Lord ask;
I declare that as a child of the most High King Our
Savior, I will remain true to the understanding that I
am under The Lord's authority and therefore, will
not get prideful;

I as a child of the most High King Our Savior Our, I will seek to do all things according to the word of The Lord;

I declare that as a child of the most High King Our Savior, I will religiously observe the laws and faithfully carry out every order given to me;

I declare that as a child of the most High King Our Savior, will observe the acts of government founded upon "In The Lord We Trust";

I declare that as a child of the most High King Our Savior, that no one is above the law of The Lord;

by signing below, I hereby declare that I will, as a child of the most High King Our Savior, from this time forward, express my love, appreciation and respect for The Lord's timetable by celebrating His appointed times, and sounding the trumpet for "Shemitah," celebrating The Lord's time of release for His people until the return of Yashyah our Savior, the author and finisher of our faith. The judge of the wicked of the earth and redeemer of the righteous for eternal rest. I honor Him by doing what I must do to help my brethren who are not yet settled;

I declare that as a child of the most High King Our Savior, I will live by the covenant obligation to strengthen the hands of others, and not seek my own welfare only, but also the welfare of others;

I declare that as a child of the most High King Our Savior, that as The Lord commanded Joshua and now commands me, calls me and is all sufficient to see me through.

I will be strong and courageous, I will not be afraid or have fear because I know The Lord is with me.

SIGNATURE

____

DATE

____

CONTACT

www.woprayerwarriors.com

EMAIL PRAYER NEEDS

w.o.prayerwarriors@gmail.com

HANDMAIDS

prepare the bride

Passover

HOLY SPRING FEAST

Weeks
Pentecost

HOLY SUMMER
FEAST

Dedication
Purim

HOLY WINTER FEAST

Tabernacles

HOLY FALL FEAST

GENERATIONS
PODCAST